THE WONDERS OF OUR WORLD

Volcanoes

Neil Morris

CRABTREE PUBLISHING COMPANY

The Wonders of our World

Crabtree Publishing Company

350 Fifth Avenue, Suite 3308 New York, New York 10118	360 York Road, R. R. 4 Niagara-on-the-Lake, Ontario Canada L0S 1J0	73 Lime Walk Headington, Oxford England 0X3 7AD

Author: Neil Morris
Managing editor: Peter Sackett
Editors: Ting Morris & David Schimpky
Designer: Richard Rowan
Production manager: Graham Darlow
Picture research: Lis Sackett

Cataloging-in-publication data

Morris, Neil
    Volcanoes

(Wonders of our world)
Includes index.
ISBN 0-86505-826-1 (library bound) ISBN 0-86505-838-5 (pbk.)
This book examines the different kinds of volcanoes and their
effects on the earth.

1. Volcanoes - Juvenile literature. I. Title. II. Series: Morris,
Neil. Wonders of our world.

QE521.3.M66 1995   j551.2'1.   LC 95-23443

© 1996 Labyrinth Publishing (UK) Ltd.
Created and Produced by Labyrinth Publishing (UK) Ltd in
conjunction with Crabtree Publishing Company.

CONTENTS

WHAT IS A VOLCANO?

A VOLCANO is an opening where molten rock and gas come from deep inside the earth. The molten rock, called magma, moves with great force through cracks in the earth's crust. The word volcano is also used to describe the mountain that is formed when magma is released. Volcanoes are named after Vulcan, the ancient Roman god of fire.

Sometimes magma flows out quietly, but occasionally volcanoes explode with great violence when they erupt.

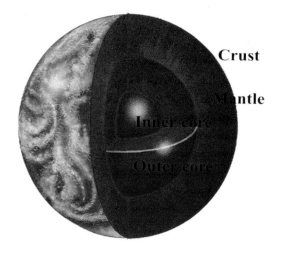

Crust

Mantle

Inner core

Outer core

BENEATH THE EARTH'S CRUST

The earth's crust is the thin layer on which we live. Beneath it is the hot mantle, from which magma comes. The outer core is made up of molten iron and nickel. At the earth's center is a solid inner core.

ERUPTION

When a volcano erupts, it often sends out gas, pieces of rock, dust, and ash, as well as magma. The magma quickly cools and forms solid rock. Lava is the name for both the magma that reaches the surface and the cooled rock. As this Icelandic volcano erupts, it spouts lava.

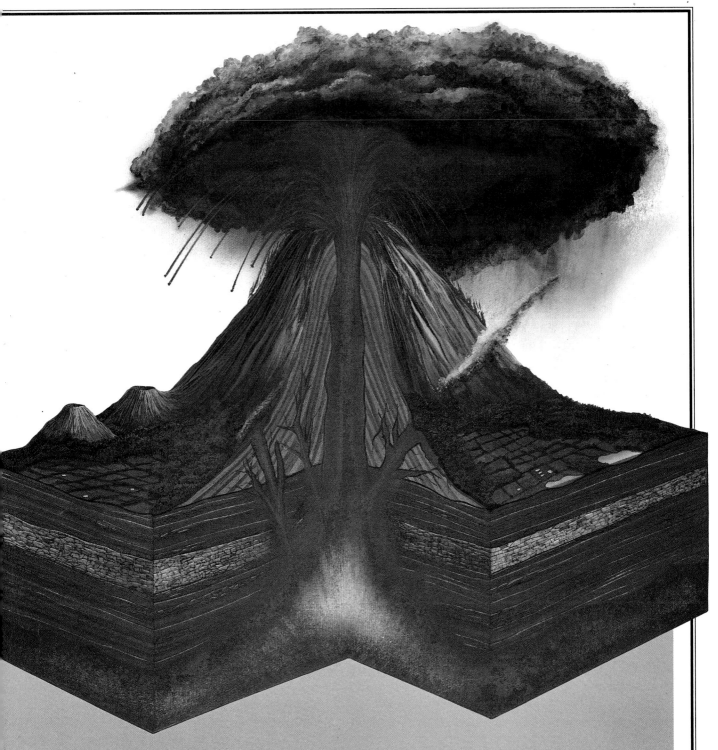

INSIDE A VOLCANO

This cross section of an erupting volcano shows red-hot lava blasting up through an opening in the earth's crust. The hole is called a vent.

Smaller side vents lead off from the main vent. The steep slope of the cone-shaped mountain is made of layers of hardened lava and ash that build up with each eruption.

WHERE IN THE WORLD?

MANY OF the world's active volcanoes lie in a huge belt around the Pacific Ocean. This belt is known as the "Ring of Fire." It runs along the edges of huge pieces of the earth's crust called plates.

Plates slowly move and rub against one another. Though they move just a tiny distance each year, their squeezing and buckling can create volcanoes and earthquakes. Many volcanoes are hidden under the oceans. Some are at oceanic ridges, where plates are moving away from one another.

THE WORLD'S VOLCANOES

Volcanoes form near the edge of plates. The Pacific Ocean lies at the center of this world map.

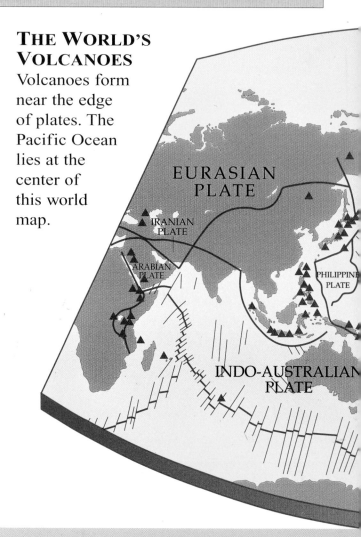

EURASIAN PLATE

IRANIAN PLATE

ARABIAN PLATE

PHILIPPINE PLATE

INDO-AUSTRALIAN PLATE

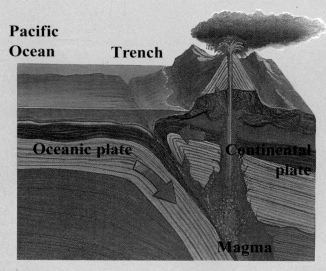

Pacific Ocean

Trench

Oceanic plate

Continental plate

Magma

RING OF FIRE VOLCANOES

Many of these cone-shaped volcanoes are on land, at the edge of the Pacific Ocean. They occur where an oceanic plate meets a continental plate. The oceanic plate is forced beneath the continental plate, which is dry land. The oceanic plate plunges into the mantle. The great heat melts the plate, and it becomes magma. The magma rises and bursts through the crust.

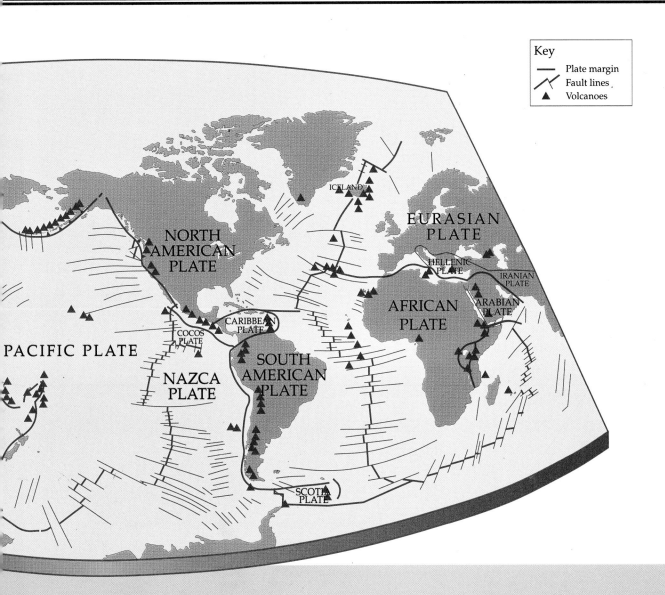

EURASIAN PLATE

NORTH AMERICAN PLATE

ICELAND

HELLENIC PLATE

IRANIAN PLATE

AFRICAN PLATE

ARABIAN PLATE

PACIFIC PLATE

CARIBBEAN PLATE

COCOS PLATE

NAZCA PLATE

SOUTH AMERICAN PLATE

SCOTIA PLATE

VOLCANOES AND EARTHQUAKES

ICELAND IS being torn in two at a rate of 2.5 centimeters (1 inch) a year, as two plates move apart. This movement makes a large crack called a fault. As the map above shows, Iceland has many volcanoes. The moving plates also create shock waves, which produce earthquakes.

DEAD OR ALIVE?

WHEN a volcano has not erupted for thousands of years, it is said to be dormant, or "sleeping." Such volcanoes may become active again. They often give off steam or have lava bubbling in their crater.

Active volcanoes may erupt at any time, and there are about 500 of these in the world. If, however, a volcano has shown no signs of activity for thousands of years, it is considered to be extinct.

WORN AWAY

MANY mountain chains were once volcanic. In the Auvergne region of France, a series of extinct volcanoes has become a chain of rounded hills. The volcanoes have been worn away by wind and rain over thousands of years.

SURPRISE ERUPTION

Sometimes volcanoes can give us a big surprise. Scientists thought that Mount Bezymyannaya, in Russia, was extinct. In 1955, however, it erupted with a massive explosion. It had actually been lying dormant.

SACRED MOUNTAIN

Mount Fuji is Japan's highest mountain, at 3776 meters (12,388 feet). Fuji is a dormant volcano. It last erupted in 1707, when it scattered ash as far away as Tokyo. It is sacred to the Ainu, the original people of Japan, and to followers of Shinto and Buddhism. People climb the mountain in July and August, when most of its snow has melted.

DIFFERENT KINDS

VOLCANOES COME in many different shapes and sizes. Lava may travel a long way before it hardens. This kind of flow forms a volcano with gently sloping sides, called a shield volcano. The largest active volcano in the world, Mauna Loa in Hawaii, is a shield volcano.

If the lava hardens before it can flow very far, it builds up high layers. Cone-shaped volcanoes, such as Mount Fuji, are created in this way, with layers of ash on top. They are sometimes called cinder cones.

FORCE OF ERUPTION

Scientists give eruptions different names. Icelandic eruptions are usually gentle. Hawaiian eruptions create rivers of lava and form shield volcanoes. Strombolian eruptions shoot out small lumps of lava, gas, and cinders. Vulcanian eruptions are even more explosive.

In destructive Peléan eruptions, avalanches of hot ash pour down the sides of the cone at high speed. These eruptions are named after Mount Pelée, a Caribbean volcano that erupted in 1902. Of the 28,000 people living in a nearby town, only two survived.

Plinian eruptions are the most explosive of all. They are named after the Roman writer, Pliny, who wrote an eyewitness account of the eruption that destroyed the ancient city of Pompeii.

ICELANDIC CRACKS

In Icelandic eruptions, runny lava flows from cracks in the earth. The cracks are up to 25 kilometers (15 miles) long, and sometimes they shoot out lava fountains. Much of the island of Iceland is made up of lava plateaus.

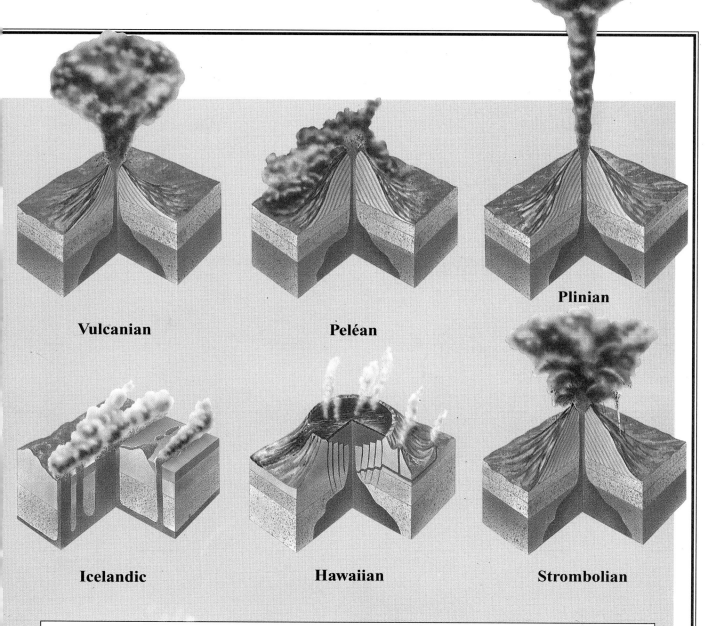

Vulcanian

Peléan

Plinian

Icelandic

Hawaiian

Strombolian

STROMBOLI

THE small volcanic island of Stromboli lies off the southwest coast of Italy. Its volcano has erupted regularly for centuries. Small explosions throw lava in the air every 15 to 30 minutes.

LAVA FLOWS

SINCE VOLCANOES erupt in different ways, the lava that is released flows in different ways too. Sometimes the lava is thrown up into the air to make spectacular fire fountains. Chunks of lava called pyroclasts may be flung out as blocks and bombs.

Some lava flows move away from volcanoes as rivers of hot rock. The longest lava flow occurred about 15 million years ago in what is now the state of Washington. The flow was 500 kilometers (311 miles) long.

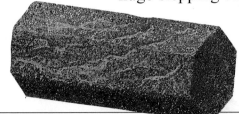

GIANT STEPPING STONES

THESE pillar-shaped rocks in Northern Ireland were formed millions of years ago when lava from a volcano cooled. The lava turned into a rock called basalt. The pillars have six sides and are over 1 meter (3 feet) high. They form what is known as the Giant's Causeway. This formation is so named because the rocks resemble huge stepping stones.

ROUGH AA

SOME lava flows have a rough, broken surface. This type of lava is known by its Hawaiian name, aa (pronounced ah-ah). Aa lava is thick and rough and breaks into chunks as the lava flow moves.

SMOOTH PAHOEHOE

Smooth lava flows are called pahoehoe (pa-hoy-hoy). The runny lava forms a skin on the surface of the flow. Sometimes pahoehoe lava continues to flow beneath the hardened surface, making a cave called a lava tube.

BOMBS AND BLOCKS

Lumps of lava cool and become solid as they fly through the air. Small, round lumps are called bombs. Larger, more angular lumps are known as blocks.

ASH AND ROCK

WHEN LAVA cools and hardens, it forms rock. The rocks that come from lava are called igneous rocks. Igneous means "fiery." There are many different igneous rocks, depending on the kind of lava and the conditions in which it flowed.

Sometimes magma does not reach the surface of the earth through volcanoes. Instead, it cools and forms igneous rocks underground. Over millions of years, these rocks may be pushed to the surface.

Volcanic ash is made up of tiny pieces of cooled lava.

BLANKET OF VOLCANIC ASH

In 1912, a huge volcanic eruption buried a vast valley in Alaska. The valley was covered in ash, up to 50 meters (160 feet) deep in places. Snow and streams, buried under the hot ash, turned to steam. The area was named Valley of Ten Thousand Smokes after the rising steam.

CONES OF ASH AND ROCK

In central Turkey, cones and pillars of rock rise from the barren landscape. Millions of years ago, a now-extinct volcano erupted, hurling out ash.

LAVA PLUG

SOMETIMES lava hardens inside a volcano. Over thousands of years, wind and rain wear away the softer rocks and leave a lava plug. This one at Le Puy, in France, is 76 meters (250 feet) high.

The ash cooled and hardened and has since been weathered by wind and rain, forming the cones. In ancient times, people cut caves into the rock for shelter.

IGNEOUS ROCKS

The most common volcanic rock is basalt, which makes up much of the solid surface of the earth. Other rocks include granite, which forms the core of many mountains, and obsidian, a dark, glassy rock. Scoria and pumice contain air holes. People use pumice to scrub their skin. Tuff is formed when ash and cinders fuse together on the ground.

Basalt **Granite**

Scoria **Pumice**

Obsidian **Tuff**

SPRINGS AND GEYSERS

SOMETIMES WATER under the ground is heated by molten rock. The water may bubble up as a hot spring, with many minerals dissolved in it.

If hot water gushes up out of the ground, we call it a geyser. The water spurts high in the air. Most geysers are in Iceland, New Zealand, and the United States. Steamboat Geyser in Wyoming is the world's tallest geyser. It shoots water up to 115 meters (377 feet) in the air.

Volcanic gases also escape through holes in the ground. We call these holes fumaroles.

OLD FAITHFUL

This geyser in Yellowstone National Park, Wyoming, earned its name by erupting very regularly. About every 66 minutes, Old Faithful shoots water and steam to a height of 46 meters (150 feet).

MUD POTS

THERE ARE many geysers in a volcanic region near Lake Rotorua, on the North Island of New Zealand. The most spectacular is a triple geyser called the Prince of Wales Feathers. Pools of boiling mud, called mud pots, are close by this geyser. Caused by leaking steam, these spectacular pools bubble and plop to make ever-changing mud patterns.

UNDER THE GROUND

A geyser has a long, vertical passage called a feeding tube. Usually several branches lead into the main feeding tube, which must be very narrow for the geyser to erupt. When the underground water boils, steam and hot water surge upwards.

MINERAL SPRINGS

At Pamukkale, in Turkey, amazing walls and terraces have been created by hot springs. The water in the springs, which bubbles on a plateau above the formation, is full of lime. The mineral deposits have built up over thousands of years to form the terraces.

AVALANCHES AND TSUNAMIS

A VOLCANIC eruption can devastate large areas surrounding the volcano. The layers of ash that pile up on the volcano may collapse and bring down part of the mountain in a huge avalanche. Heavy rain or melted snow from the top of a mountain can turn the avalanche into a mud flow.

An eruption near or beneath the sea can cause giant waves called tsunamis. These waves travel very fast across oceans. At sea, they can capsize ships. When tsunamis reach shore, they damage coastal towns.

TSUNAMI DAMAGE

These fishing boats were thrown onto land by a tsunami that hit the Alaska coast. Tsunamis are sometimes called "tidal waves," but they have nothing to do with tides.

ASH AND LAVA

IN 1973, an erupting volcano threatened a fishing town on Heimaey, a small island off the coast of Iceland. A thick, steaming lava flow almost destroyed the harbor. Much of the island was buried under ash.

**Krakatoa
1883**

**Anak Krakatoa
1994**

CHILD OF KRAKATOA

In 1883, the volcanic island of Krakatoa, in Indonesia, erupted. The explosion destroyed two-thirds of the island and was heard nearly 5000 kilometers (3100 miles) away. It caused a massive tsunami. The waves killed over 36,000 people living on Java and Sumatra. In 1927, a new volcanic island appeared. It is called Anak Krakatoa, or "Child of Krakatoa."

ANCIENT ERUPTION

OUNT VESUVIUS, on the Bay of Naples in southern Italy, had been dormant for 800 years. Then suddenly, on August 24, AD 79, it blew out a plug of lava and rocketed tons of lava, pumice, and ash into the sky. A thick blanket of ash soon buried the nearby town of Pompeii. Further along the coast, the town of Herculaneum was also buried—under 13 meters (43 feet) of boiling mud.

VESUVIUS

ESUVIUS has erupted many times since AD 79. The last eruption was in 1944. Over the centuries a new cone has formed on the south side of the volcano. In this photo, part of the old crater can be seen in the background.

EXCAVATION

In 1860, an archaeologist named Giuseppe Fiorelli began to excavate Pompeii. He invented a method that showed how the townspeople died. Fiorelli pumped wet plaster of Paris into the spaces taken up by bodies. After the plaster hardened, he dug the casts out of the volcanic rock.

PLASTER CASTS

WHEN they were dug out, the plaster casts showed adults trying to save themselves and protect their children. A dog was also found, tethered by a chain to its bronze collar.

DAY OF DESTRUCTION

Although there had been earth tremors for four days, the citizens of Pompeii were caught by surprise when Mount Vesuvius erupted. The blast sent people running into the streets.

A column of smoke rose from the volcano, and a cloud headed for the town. Pompeii was soon buried under 5 meters (16 feet) of ash and pumice. Thousands of people died in the town and in the surrounding countryside.

A NEW ISLAND IS BORN

IN 1963, fishermen off the coast of Iceland saw smoke rising from the sea. They thought a ship was on fire. In fact, it was steam caused by an erupting volcano under the sea. By the next day, the volcano had formed a small island, which was named Surtsey.

Volcanic islands often form above very hot areas, called hot spots, in the earth's mantle. The Hawaiian islands were formed over hot spots.

SURTSEY SURFACES
Surtsey's birth began when two plates on the floor of the Atlantic Ocean moved apart. This movement caused a volcanic eruption. Steam billowed up from the surface of the sea (above), as water came in contact with the hot rock.

NEW LIFE

SEEDS SOON reached Surtsey, carried by the wind or by birds. They produced grasses and flowers. Before long, sea birds started nesting among the rocks. By 1980 there was a whole breeding colony on the island.

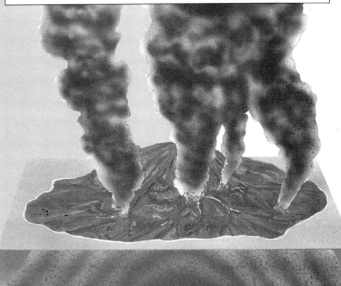

When the top of the volcano rose above the surface of the sea, lava and ash exploded out of the vent (above). A new island was born. Lava fountains and lava flows built up the island for several months (right). Then, a second vent started throwing lava on the island. Small eruptions continued for four years, and the island grew to a height of 174 meters (570 feet) above sea level. The new island was named Surtsey, after Surtur, the Norse god of fire.

A MOUNTAIN EXPLODES

MOUNT ST. Helens lies in the Cascade Mountains in Washington state. The Cascades are near the Pacific coast, so they are part of the world's "Ring of Fire."

In March of 1980, after lying dormant for 123 years, Mount St. Helens shook itself awake with a series of earthquakes. A bulge appeared high on the mountain and began to grow at the rate of more than 1 meter (3 feet) a day. Suddenly, on May 18, the volcano erupted with a huge explosion that blew apart the top of the mountain.

BEFORE AND AFTER

Mount St. Helens looked beautiful and peaceful before it erupted (below left). On May 18, 1980, a cloud of ash spouted from the top of the mountain (below). An avalanche ran down the side of the cone. Seconds later, a huge explosion blew 400 meters (1312 feet) off the height of the mountain. Huge chunks of rock were hurled out. The mountain was left with an enormous crater (right).

DEVASTATION

GASES BOILED out of the open volcano for nine hours. Clouds of ash were sent high into the sky, and mud flows poured down the side of the cone. Volcanic ash and rock fragments fell on 550 square kilometers (212 square miles) of surrounding forest. Tall trees were totally flattened by the blast, and 57 people in the area were killed.

VOLCANIC BENEFITS

VOLCANOES CAN be very destructive to humans and to the environment. Yet, volcanoes also have advantages and bring many benefits to people. Geothermal energy—heat from beneath the earth's surface—is one benefit. This kind of energy creates very little pollution.

We also use volcanic rocks in various ways. Granite is a good building material. Pumice is used as a cleaning product. Valuable gemstones, such as diamonds and opals, are found embedded in igneous rock.

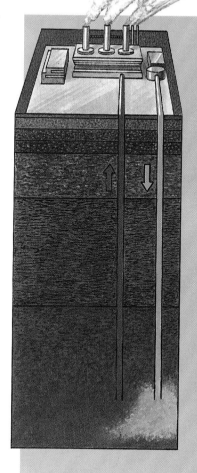

GEOTHERMAL ENERGY

Volcanic rocks contain heat from the earth, or geothermal energy. Holes are drilled into volcanic rock to release the hot water held in its cracks. When the hot water reaches the surface, its steam is used to turn turbines and make electricity. In some power plants, cold water is pumped down into the volcanic rock to be heated.

FERTILE SOIL

VOLCANIC ash is full of nutrients that enrich soil. If the ash is too deep, it will kill plants, but a thin covering is a good thing for farmers. Mount Etna, on the Italian island of Sicily, is the largest volcano in Europe, and it erupts regularly. The lower slopes of Etna and the nearby countryside are very fertile farmland. Oranges and lemons are among the fruits grown in this area.

CONSTANT HOT WATER

Iceland has thousands of hot springs and many geothermal power plants. Water from these springs is piped into homes to provide hot water and heating. In Iceland's cold climate, geothermal energy is used to heat greenhouses so that vegetables and fruit may be grown. Icelanders can also swim outdoors all year round.

Diamond

Opal

Ruby

Saphire

Aquamarine

Beryl

Moonstone

Topaz

Zircon

PRECIOUS STONES

VALUABLE MINERALS are often found in igneous rocks. Diamonds and opals are some of the mineral crystals, or gemstones, that are mined. When molten rock meets impure limestone deep in the earth, it changes the limestone into marble. The impurities that are present may then form rubies and sapphires.

TODAY AND TOMORROW

ALMOST 2000 years after the great eruption of Vesuvius, over 2 million people live in its shadow in the Bay of Naples. Volcanoes are a natural feature of our planet. We cannot stop them, but we can learn more about them. Volcanologists—scientists who study volcanoes—make new discoveries all the time.

We can learn to live more safely in danger zones. One way to do this is to find ways of predicting when disaster might strike.

PROBING FOR KNOWLEDGE

Volcanologists wear special protective clothing to lower probes into volcanoes and take lava and gas samples. Their heat-reflecting, insulated suits offer protection, but the work is still dangerous.

DIVERTING LAVA

SCIENTISTS are discovering how to use barriers to divert lava flows and protect towns and people. In 1992, concrete blocks were dropped near lava from Mount Etna for this purpose.

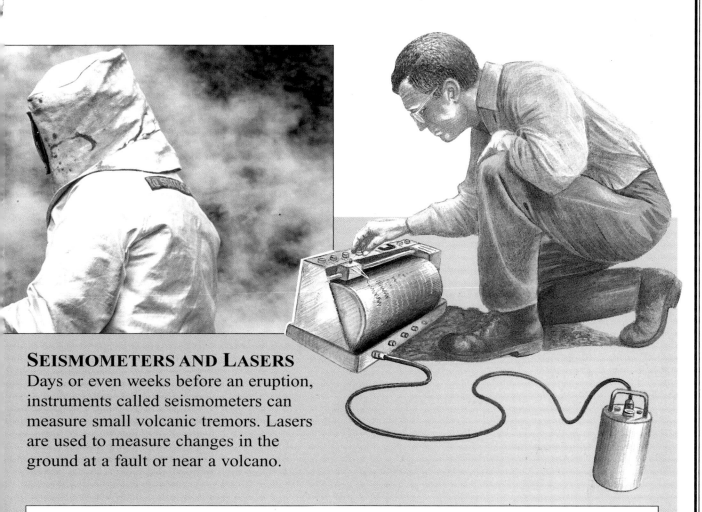

SEISMOMETERS AND LASERS

Days or even weeks before an eruption, instruments called seismometers can measure small volcanic tremors. Lasers are used to measure changes in the ground at a fault or near a volcano.

OBSERVING VOLCANOES

CENTERS such as this observatory in Naples (right) help us learn more about volcanoes. Another scientific base on Hawaii is constantly on the lookout for any volcanic activity.

GLOSSARY

Aa   A thick, rough type of lava that breaks into chunks.

Avalanche   A large fall of rocks or snow down a mountainside.

Basalt   The most common volcanic rock.

Crater   A bowl-shaped opening at the top of a volcano.

Crust   The hard outer layer of the earth.

Dormant   Describing a volcano that is "sleeping" but may become active again.

Erupt   To throw out rocks, gases, and other material.

Excavate   To dig in the ground to find information about the past.

Extinct   No longer active or dormant; dead.

Fault   A fracture in the earth's surface.

Fumarole   A hole in the ground that releases volcanic gases and steam.

Geothermal   Describing heat inside the earth.

Geyser   A spring that shoots out hot water.

Granite   An igneous rock widely used for building.

Hawaiian   Describing a volcanic eruption that creates rivers of lava.

Hot spot   A very hot part of the earth's mantle, which forms volcanic islands.

Icelandic   Describing a volcanic eruption in which the lava flow is gentle.

Igneous   Describing rocks made from solidified lava on the earth's surface, or from magma that cools inside the earth.

Lava   Molten rock that pours out of a volcano.

Magma	Molten rock formed in the earth's mantle.
Mantle	The thick layer of rock beneath the earth's crust.
Molten	Describing something that has been melted.
Obsidian	A dark, glassy igneous rock.
Pahoehoe	A smooth, runny type of lava.
Peléan	Describing a volcanic eruption with avalanches of hot ash.
Plate	A slowly moving piece of the earth's crust; the earth's plates fit together like a giant jigsaw puzzle.
Plateau	A flat area of high land.
Plinian	Describing the most explosive volcanic eruptions.
Pumice	A light, smooth igneous rock full of air holes.
Pyroclast	A chunk of solid lava thrown out during a volcanic eruption.
Scoria	A rough, heavy igneous rock full of air holes.
Seismometer	An instrument that records earth tremors.
Strombolian	Describing a volcanic eruption that shoots lava, gas, and cinders.
Tsunami	A giant wave caused by a volcanic eruption or an earthquake.
Tuff	An igneous rock formed by ash and cinders fusing on the ground.
Vent	An opening in the earth's crust through which lava and gases escape.
Volcanologist	A scientist who studies volcanoes.
Vulcanian	Describing an explosive volcanic eruption.

INDEX

A
aa lava 13
active volcanoes 6, 8
Anak Krakatoa 19
ash 5, 10, 14-15, 18, 20, 21, 23, 24, 25, 26
Auvergne region 8
avalanches 18, 24

B
basalt rock 12, 15
blocks 12, 13
bombs 12, 13

C
Cascade mountains 24
caves 13, 15
cones 14, 15
core 4
cracks 4, 7, 10
crust 4, 5, 6

D
dormant volcanoes 8, 9, 20, 24

E
earthquakes 6, 7
eruptions 4, 5, 8, 9, 10-11, 14, 17, 18, 20, 21
extinct volcanoes 8, 9, 14

F
faults 7
Fiorelli, Guiseppe 20, 21
fumaroles 16

G
gases, volcanic 16
gemstones 26, 27
geothermal energy 26, 27
geysers 16-17
Giant's Causeway 12

H
Herculaneum 20
hot spots 22
hot springs 16, 17, 27

I
Iceland 7, 10, 16, 18, 22, 27
igneous rocks 14-15, 27

K
Krakatoa 19

L
Lake Rotorua 16
lasers 29
lava 4, 5, 10, 11, 12-13, 14, 15, 18, 20, 22, 23, 28
lava plug 15
lava tube 13

M
magma 4, 5, 6, 14
mantle 4, 6, 22
Mauna Loa 10
Mount Bezymyannaya 9
Mount Etna 26
Mount Fuji 9, 10
Mount Pelée 10
Mount St. Helens 24-25
Mount Vesuvius 20-21

mud flows 18, 20, 25
mud pots 16

O
observatories 29
Old Faithful geyser 16

P
Pacific Ocean 6
pahoehoe lava 13
Pamukkale mineral deposits 17
pillars 12, 14
plates 6, 7, 22
Pompeii 20-21
pyroclasts 12, 20, 21, 24

R
Ring of Fire 6, 24

S
seismometers 29
shield volcano 10
Steamboat Geyser 16
Stromboli 11
Surtsey 22-23

T
tsunamis 18-19

V
Valley of Ten Thousand Smokes 14
vents 5, 23
volcanic rocks 12, 13, 14-15, 20, 24, 25, 26, 27
volcanologists 28

123456789 Printed in the U.S.A. 432109876

DATE DUE

40.5811